Foundation Curriculum
Copyright © 2014
Written by Linda D. Washington
Illustrated by Rebeca Flott
Edited by Joyce S. Pace and Rita K. Jeffries

STORY BOOK LESSON 5
"YOUR POWER IN JESUS"

Jesus told us to pray and say,
"And lead us not into temptation,
but deliver us from the Evil One."

Let's see why Jesus wants you to pray not to be tempted,
and to save you from the evil one!

When you chose to believe Jesus, Father made you new in your spirit. But guess what did not become new?

The way you think and the words you say did not become new.

When God made the heavens and earth He spoke good words that gave everything life.

Father made you to be like Him and to show His Kingdom on earth. So He put spirit power in every word you speak. Your good words are filled with life. But your bad words are filled with death.

Whenever you say words that God has said, you are speaking God's good words. God's words send out the good power of life, and God's words make good things happen.

But when you say words that God did not say, those are the words filled with the power of death. Those are words that the devil likes. Whenever the devil hears words that are NOT what God has said, he can use the power in those words to cause the bad and evil thing to happen.

This is how the power in your words works. Has anyone ever said something mean or bad about you?

How did it make you feel?
It does not feel good when mean words are said about you.

Do you remember what Jesus said to do when people listen to the devil, and say bad things?

Jesus told you to pray for them.

Has anyone ever said something good about you?
How did the good words make you feel?
Good words make you feel good inside. The power in the good words cause life to come inside of you.

God gave you the power to choose the words you say. You can say words that help others. Or you could say words that hurt others.

Father wants you to know why you should use your power to THINK and SAY good words.

Satan, the devil is the evil one. The battle on earth is with him and his demons. He does not fight you by hitting or pushing you. The fight with him and his demons is spiritual. Spirit things are things you cannot see. The devil tries to get you to THINK bad thoughts so he can begin to trick you! But you must remember Jesus has already won. And you have the super power of Holy Spirit inside of you that is BIGGER and GREATER than all the power of the evil one!

Listen closely so you will know how the enemy fights and Holy Spirit can help you beat him every time.

First, the devil tries to get you to THINK a
bad thought.

If he can get you to think the bad thing, next he tries
to get you to SAY WORDS about the bad thought. He
knows that he can lead you to death with words that
go against God's Words. Finally he wants you to think
it is alright to do the bad thing.

Jesus called the devil a thief who comes to steal, kill
and destroy you. The thief wants to steal God's Word
so you will choose to say bad things that God
did not say.

Now you can see how the evil one tries to trick you.
He brings a bad thought and tells lies for you to think
about, just like he told Adam and Eve.

But Father has put awesome life and power in His Words. And when you, as God's ambassador, say the same words that God has said, Holy Spirit makes God's Words come out of your mouth like a spirit sword.

God's Word is like a sword with two sides. This is how your sword works when you say God's good Words.

One side of the sword cuts holes into the evil one and makes him run away from you fast. The other side of the sword makes you stronger because the good Words of God that you said made the power of life come inside of you!

Did you know that you can make bad thoughts leave?

Father gave you power to think about whatever YOU CHOOSE to think about!

You could choose to think about a little blue monkey holding a yellow banana. The monkey has a long tail. He grabs the branch with his hand and swings from tree to tree. He makes monkey sounds. Can you make a sound like a monkey?

The monkey is so funny. You can see the monkey in your mind when you choose to think about it. But you did not have to think about the monkey if you did not want to. Do you understand?

You can change whatever you are thinking to a different thought just by choosing to think of something different.

The devil can't make you think bad thoughts. You know his tricks, and he can't lie to you!

Did you know that Jesus had another secret weapon he used on earth?

Jesus used the weapon of prayer! Prayer is talking and being with Father. Because you are God's child and ambassador, Jesus gave you a doorway to come into Father's GREAT throne room any time you choose.

To enter God's throne room, go to a private place to be alone. Then think about how very good God is, and how much He loves you. Think about how Father always wants to help you. Then open your mouth and say words of thanks and praise to God your Father. You could choose to pray in God's language of tongues and Holy Spirit will help you. Say words that you really mean from your heart.

You can sing Him a song you know, or sing Him a new song that you made up. When you thank and praise God from your heart, the Spirit of Jesus leads you to Father's throne. You can climb up on Father's lap, love Him, and talk with Him.

Father and Jesus are waiting for you.

You must remember and know that Jesus has already saved you from all the powers of the evil one. Jesus has given you weapons to use on earth to make you dangerous to the enemy. Jesus is the door for God's children and ambassadors to go to their Father's throne room and pray. Prayer is your secret weapon!

Your greatest power is Holy Spirit in you. For it is Holy Spirit that puts power in the sword of God's Word for you whenever you say what God your Father says. This is what Father has said about you.

You are His child.
You are blessed.
You can come boldly into His throne room anytime and He will help you.
You are a king and an ambassador in Jesus.

Here's your homework.
Keep learning what God says.
Then say what God has said, just like Jesus!

The Purpose of the Foundation Curriculum

To firmly establish God's truth in each child's heart early in life so they will understand and know God's love and choose to live fully in the victory that Jesus Christ has already won.

The Goals

To show God's children his love, their true identity as children of God, their authority and power in Christ Jesus, their helper Holy Spirit, and how to pray to their Father in heaven.

YOUR POWER IN JESUS

Story Book Lesson 5

The Objectives to understand from "Your Power in Jesus" are:

1. You have the power to choose to think new like Jesus.

2. Father spoke good Words and made all things come alive.

3. You can choose to speak good words like Father.

4. Your words have the power of death and life in them.

5. The devil tries to trick you to say bad words that you may think.

6. Father gave you power to change any bad thought to good.

7. You can speak Father's Word and it will cut like a sword.

8. You can pray and go boldly into your Father's throne room any time.

P.A.C.E.

Products and Activities
for Christian Education

For Free Follow-Up Activities to Reinforce This Story Book Lesson Please Visit
www.ABC-Jesus.com

Biblical quotes were from different versions of the holy Bible.

www.ingramcontent.com/pod-product-compliance
Lightning Source LLC
Chambersburg PA
CBHW041559040426
42447CB00002B/232